CW00810937

Disclaimer
Mountain biking and training for mountain biking are potentially dangerous. Race Line Publishing, the author and their representatives assume no liability whatsoever for any damages associated in any way with the information contained herein.

Before you start any workout program, check with your physician. If you have any questions or concerns, consult a qualified trainer near you.

www.leelikesbikes.com

This book is dedicated to my wife Arlette and our kids Kate (23), Ian (20), Finley (3) and Fiona (3) — who all keep me fully pinned.

No rest days around here!

-- Lee

Big thanks to:

- **Specialized:** My Stumpjumper 29 Carbon with Roval carbon trail wheels rips all terrain, from pump/jump to XC and light DH. What a capable, versatile machine.

- **FOX:** Reliable and dialed suspension. Try the 34 on your trail bike.

- **Shimano:** Confidence-inspiring cockpit, drivetrain and brakes. Once you experience XTR Trail brakes, you'll demand them on all of your bikes.

- **RallySport Health and Fitness:** Stability, strength, power and hopefully longevity courtesy of master trainer Erin Carson.

CONTENTS

This program will help you ride better, faster and, if you want, gnarlier. Tim Moore applies power on Holy Cross Trail in Grand Junction, CO. Chris Quinn with the spot. Photo by yannphotovideo.com

WHY ARE WE DOING THIS?

The stronger you are —sitting, standing, pedaling, pumping, cornering and just plain ripping — the better you'll feel, the longer you'll be able to ride, the faster you'll ride and the more fun you'll have.

PUMP UP THE BASE:
Rock the trainer this winter.
Rock the trails this summer.

A 12-week plan to:
• Improve your pedaling skills and power
• Ride faster and easier on all terrain
• Train quickly and efficiently
http://www.leelikesbikes.com/pump-up-the-base-book-and-training-program.html

We want to be as strong and fit as we can, without ruining the rest of our lives. To get the most out of riding, we need a plan.

Well, you don't *need* a plan. You can ride whenever and however you want. That's fine if you have lots of time and you don't mind semi-sucking. If you want to be the best you can be — and save time and energy for work, family and life — a plan really helps.

Fact is, smart riders can ride less and still pin it on the weekends. It's all about the structured mid-week workouts.

This program picks up where Pump Up the Base ends. By now you should have decent overall fitness and be ready to step it up. The main tool for improvement is a progression of short, intense intervals. You should do many of these pedaling. If you are a real Rider (capital R), you'll do some of them on a pump track or real terrain.

This program focuses on maximizing the amount of power you can sustain while pedaling, pumping and just plain ripping.

Among other things, this program will:

- Encourage you to go harder than normal on some days
- Give you permission to take it easy on other days.

You see, most of us do our easy rides too hard and our hard rides too easy. We end up riding in a kind of half-@$$ed middle ground that tires us out but doesn't let us reach our full potential.

Do your most satisfying bike moments happen when you're cruising? No way. They happen when you're pinning it so fast you lose track of yourself and reach a Flow (capital F) state. That's the magic we're all looking for, and the more skilled, strong and fit we are, the more flow we'll find.

Prerequisite work

You should have at least 8-10 weeks of riding two to three days per week: lots of easy miles plus some playing around at the higher intensities. If you just finished the Pump Up the Base program, you are ready to rock. Be sure to take an easy week or two between programs.

Meet your trainer

The clever and mighty Lester Pardoe is a Coaching Specialist at the Boulder Center for Sports Medicine. He and his colleagues work with riders of all levels, including the fastest of the fast.

Lester is an expert-level XC ripper/racer and a three-time Olympic qualifier in speed skating. A former World Championship and Olympic coach for speed skating, Lester is a certified coach in cycling, speed skating, triathlon and ice hockey.

Lester knows his stuff, and Lee thanks him for sharing his knowledge.

To work with Lester in person or remotely, email him at LPardoe@bch.org
 www.bouldersportsmedicine.org

Lester gets it done at La Ruta de Los Conquistadores stage race in Costa Rica.

THE MISSION

Prepare to Pin It is a simple, flexible system for early and mid-season training. It will help you gain the most overall mountain bike fitness with the least amount of time and training stress.

This sort of group climb is more gratifying at the front. Chris LeGault leads Chris Quinn in Allens Park, CO. Photo by yannphotovideo.com.

This program uses a complete approach to cycling fitness that covers all levels of pedaling intensity and acknowledges the importance of bike-handling skill and strength (crazy: a training program that realizes riders like to Ride). It includes three training options — Pinner, Turbo and Ripper — each of which can be further tweaked to your needs.

Prepare to Pin It will be useful for many types of riders:

- Everyone who wants to have more fun on their rides. Try the "Pinner" option.

- Anyone who wants to "step it up" this year. Show your buddies who's boss. Start with the "Pinner" option.

- Cross-country and endurance racers who want a proven program. Many racers get into over-complicated training plans. This one is simple and repeatable. Try the "Turbo" option.

- Enduro and gravity racers who need to develop their full riding abilities. This program can be tweaked for shorter, harder events such as dual slalom. Try the "Ripper" option and do a lot of your intervals at the pump track, BMX track or real terrain.

- You: Especially if you have a busy life but still want to pin it.

Specific benefits

More specifically, when you Pin It you will:

- Teach your body to make more lactate, learn to function with more lactate and get rid of lactate faster.

- Make even higher short-term (anaerobic) power, and sustain it longer.

- Achieve even higher max power.

- Recover more quickly from very hard efforts.

- Maintain a higher overall pace, and sustain it longer.

- Solidify the foundation of your aerobic engine.

- Get quality rest so you can pin it another day.

Plus, you'll build on the good stuff you hopefully started in Pump Up the Base:

- Build aerobic capacity, neuromuscular power and neuromuscular coordination.

- Learn to pedal more smoothly and powerfully both in and out of the saddle

- Increase your top cadence

- Broaden your powerband

- Stress your body enough to make you improve, but not beat you down

- Use your time very efficiently

Steve Lacey lays down the anaerobic power in Moab, UT. In a situation like this, fitness can make the difference between being stoked and injured. Photo by yannphotovideo.com.

What's different about this approach?

First of all, you get Lester Pardoe. Do you already have a top-level, elite trainer? Well, now you do. Lester works with riders of all styles and levels — including the most elite of the elite — at the Boulder Center for Sports Medicine. Importantly, he works with normal people like us. People with busy lives who just want to rip it up.

Second, this program covers all aspects of riding fitness, from very easy to very hard, in a way that creates a well-rounded mountain bike rider. Whether you want to cruise epic adventures, hammer a weekend ride, rally an enduro or slay a downhill run, this program will will give you a structure to work with.

Third, it shows you how to apply proven training protocols to real riding skills. If you can perform some of your intervals on a pump track or real terrain, you'll have a huge advantage over the dirt roadies — and you'll have way more fun.

Mountain biking requires a whole lot more than sit-and-spin fitness. Doug Mers powers up Devil's Backbone Trail in Loveland, CO. What a great place for some real-world climbing intervals. Photo by yannphotovideo.com.

Don't suck at recovery

Lots of people train really well — it's easy to ride a lot and beat yourself up — but they suck at recovery. The trick is to find the perfect balance where you get enough rest to recover and get stronger, but not so much rest you don't improve.

• Pay attention to your body.

• Experiment. Find your own balance.

• When in doubt, rest.

Resting is hard to do — especially when you really love to pin it!

Make it yours

This is a system, an approach, rather than a precise program. If you follow these protocols, you'll be in great all-around shape.

• If you want to ride longer, put in more easy time between your hard times.

• If you want to ride faster, go very hard in the hard sessions. But don't overlook the easy rides; they help you recover, and they build endurance.

• If you want to excel at a certain type of event — ultra endurance, XC, Enduro, DH or gated racing — focus on the duration and intensity levels of your race.

• No matter who you are, mix in all types of workouts. If you follow this protocol, you'll be ready for just about anything.

As a skills instructor, I need to hang with elite cross country racers and triathletes, as well as fast gravity racers and BMXers. This approach helps me do that — even though I'm 44 with four kids and three jobs, and I have less riding time than ever.

TRAINING SCIENCE 101

This is not a physiology textbook, but we need to cover some basics. This will help you understand what types of training we do, how they all fit together and why they are important. Also, you'll understand what all the bike nerds are talking about.

You might not think of it while you're struggling up the Left Hand Canyon OHV area in Boulder, CO, but climbing tests your threshold power — and your ability to punch above it on the really steep sections. Sean Buckman, Dave Chase and Chad Melis (single speed!) pedal where most ride motos. Photo by yannphotovideo.com.

Threshold power

This is the amount of power you can sustain for a long time. Threshold power is the main determinant of how fast you can rip a trail ride or XC race.

The classic test is average power for an hour. The more humane test is average power for 20 minutes. If you have access to a power meter, warm up then give yourself a test. This number will be used to calculate your various training levels.

If you don't have a power meter, you can go by heart rate. Warm up thoroughly then do two 20-minute efforts with 5-10 minutes rest between them. Lester says your average heart rate for the second effort will be very close to your threshold heart rate.

> During hard efforts (Level 4 and harder), your heart rate might not respond quickly enough to reflect the amount of work you're doing, so it might seem too low at first. Don't worry: If you're doing long or multiple intervals, your heart will catch up with the workload.

If you don't have a heart rate monitor, you can go by feel.

110%

In general, your average power for 20 minutes is 110-113% of your average power for 60 minutes. That is, if you can average 200 watts for 20 minutes, you'll probably average about 180 watts for an hour.

On the following pages are the commonly accepted intensity levels.

Our photographer Yann Ropars is one of those strong climbers who can ride to the front of the group, take photos then get back in front again. Here he finds balance on Ginny Trail in Fort Collins, CO.

Intensity levels

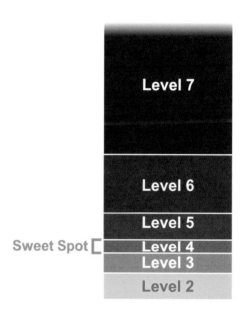

Level 7

Level 6

Level 5

Sweet Spot [Level 4

Level 3

Level 2

Level 1

Level 1 – Active Recovery

Power: <55% of threshold power

Heart rate: <68% of threshold heart rate

Feel: Very easy. Just walking around.

Level 2 – Endurance

Power: 56-75% of threshold power

Heart rate: 69-83% of threshold heart rate

Feel: Easy conversational pace. Not tired after your ride, unless it's very long.

Level 3 – Tempo

Power: 76-90% of threshold power

Heart rate: 84-94% of threshold heart rate

Feel: Moderate effort. You can talk, but you're breathing hard. You can keep riding for a long while, but it's tiring. If you're out riding by yourself, having fun but not trying to crush it, you'll likely end up here.

Level 4 – Lactate Subthreshold (aka Sweet Spot)

Power: 91-100% of threshold power

Heart rate: 95-100% of threshold heart rate

Feel: Medium-hard. Orange-red. You can talk, but only in short sentences. At this level you're going hard but not killing yourself. "That's what makes it sweet," says Lester.

Level 4, aka Sweet Spot, is a great place to train your aerobic (endurance) ability. You get a whole lot of benefit for relatively little punishment.

Level 5 – Suprathreshold

Power: 101-115% of threshold power

Heart rate: >101% of threshold heart rate

Feel: You can only keep this up for a few minutes. Oh man, this is hard. When's it gonna be over?

Level 6 – VO2 Max

Power: >116% of threshold power

Heart rate: Not applicable at first because the effort is so hard and short.

Feel: Very hard. Near maximal effort. Super uncomfortable after less than a minute. I hate my life!

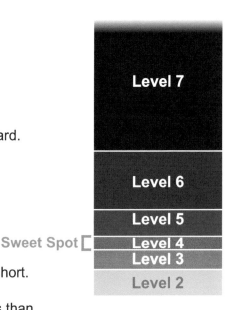

Level 7

Level 6

Level 5

Sweet Spot [Level 4

Level 3

Level 2

Level 1

Level 7 – Neuromuscular power

Power: Max power. Full gas. GO!
You can train neuromuscular power with pure all-out sprinting and short Level 5 and 6 efforts.

Heart rate: Not applicable because the effort is so hard and short.

Feel: If you're fresh, it requires focus but does not hurt. If you're tired, it's very, very uncomfortable.

Real mountain biking — the kind we all love or aspire to do — requires a lot of sprinting, hopping and other explosive movement. The only way to train this … is to practice it. Chris Quinn goes Level 7 at Curt Gowdy State Park, WY. Photo by yannphotovideo.com.

Mixing it up

A major goal of this program is to make you a well-rounded rider who can handle long rides, hard climbs and the occasional power moves. This means working the full range of intensity levels, with special focus on the levels that will help you the most and hurt you the least.

Here are the levels we will focus on, and why.

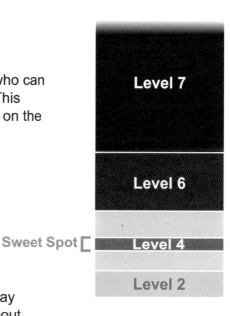

Level 1 (light yellow)

Resting and rebuilding. Remember that hard work breaks your body down. Rest builds it up stronger. Rest is important!

On your off days, take a very easy ride or a walk with your kids. Play at the park. Do something to stay loose, but remember today is about resting (and having a life).

Level 2 (yellow)

This is classic long, easy base training. Traditional Level 2 rides are two to six hours long.

While some trainers say Level 2 isn't very important, and that you can perform well with only higher-level work, Lester says Level 2 provides some very real benefits:

- It increases your red blood cell count. Think of Level 2 as affordable, legal EPO.

- It increases the size and density of your mitochondria, which are the energy centers of your cells.

- It increases your blood volume and the density of the capillaries. Denser capillary networks deliver more oxygen to working muscles. Greater blood volume helps you handle long, hot days (this is important for everyone, including downhillers who have slalom and downhill practice on the same hot day at Sea Otter).

- At Level 2 you burn more fat than at higher levels. This can help you lose weight, and it helps you access an almost unlimited store of energy. Well, Lee has an unlimited store of energy.

- When you train at Level 2, you teach your body to burn more fat at all intensity levels. This means you can ride harder and longer without bonking. This is essential for endurance riders. Plus you can lose that baby weight.

- Level 2 yields similar training benefits as Level 3, but it's less tiring. Less tired is better.

Level 2 training might not be exciting, but it builds the foundation for greater power and endurance at the higher levels.

Do not skip the Level 2 work!

Hide the Level 2

Lester says you should fit in as much Level 2 training as your schedule and body can handle. Lee says you don't have to grind out six-hour road rides every weekend. You'll end up miserable and maybe divorced.

All Level 2 work counts: long rides, short rides, warm ups, cool downs, rests between intervals, cruising to the top of the slalom track, pushing up DH runs, riding for groceries, mellow pump/DJ sessions, cornering drills ...

As long as you keep moving at a moderate pace, you can fit in a lot of Level 2 riding without chaining yourself to the road bike all day.

Lee: I simply don't have time or patience for long, easy rides. I fit a fair amount of Level 2 into my commuting, training and coaching, and I'm able to hang for a few hours. If you need to ride longer than that, you need more Level 2.

Shoot for at least 55% of your riding time to be in Level 2. During the winter, that should be more like 65%.

Sweet Spot (orange-red)

The "sweet spot" at the low end of Level 4, just below your threshold, gives you the most efficient development of your aerobic system, with the least amount of training stress.

Sweet spot training helps you sustain a higher long-term pace, for longer. This is the bread and butter of cycling. It's how you get around on your bike.

Pump Up the Base contained tons of sweet spot work. This program contains enough to keep you sharp.

Casual group ride in a beautiful place: Relax in Level 2 and know you're burning fat. Coyote Ridge Trail in Fort Collins, CO. Photo by yannphotovideo.com

Level 6 (red)

Red intervals increase your anaerobic capacity, which is your ability to generate very high power for short periods, hold it longer then recover faster.

Higher anaerobic capacity helps many areas of mountain biking, including:

- Steep, technical climbs

- Powering through water, mud, gravel, sand and snow

- Fast, rough descents

- Aggressive downhill runs

- 4X, dual slalom and pump track action

- Long sets of big dirt jumps

- Passing other riders

- Pretty much pinning it!

Level 7 (black)

This trains your nerves and muscles to GO! If you don't develop and practice awesome power, you will not have awesome power when you want it.

Level 7 sprints are short: five to six seconds full out. Go HARD or don't go.

The higher your max is, the smoother and more efficient you are at lower levels. If you can sprint at 200 rpm and 1,500 watts, 120 rpm and 500 watts up that steep hill ain't nothin'.

But what about Levels 3 and 5?

Like we've said elsewhere in this book, most riders spend too much time going medium (in Level 3). That gives them all the fatigue of riding a lot, but only some of the fitness.

We are going to train endurance in the Level 4 Sweet Spot, and we'll use the right amount of Levels 6 and 7 to push your higher-level capacity.

"99 percent of riders ride at too moderate a pace," said Rob Pickels, an exercise physiologist at Boulder Center for Sports Medicine. "They need to polarize their training."

Polarized training will make you more fast — not just more tired.

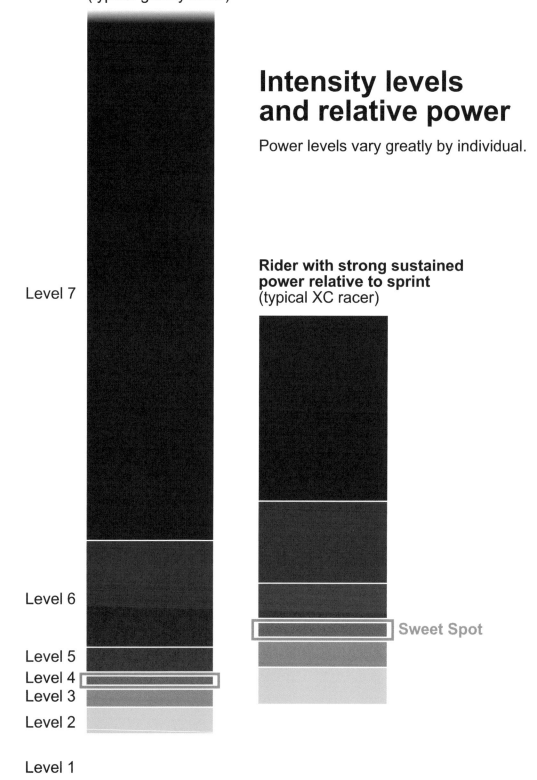

**Rider with strong sprint
relative to sustained power**
(typical gravity racer)

Intensity levels
and relative power

Power levels vary greatly by individual.

**Rider with strong sustained
power relative to sprint**
(typical XC racer)

Level 7

Sweet Spot

Level 6

Level 5
Level 4
Level 3
Level 2

Level 1

WHAT YOU'LL BE DOING

This program features two to three targeted sessions per week that work specific areas of fitness.

In addition to these prescribed workouts, you'll be ripping sick weekend rides, taking easy days and having a life.

You know you want to ride this section! Crossing the Continental Divide in Colorado is always going to be hard, but some smart training will make it less horrible. Photo by yannphotovideo.com

This 12-week program includes:

3 rest/test weeks

These relatively easy weeks contain easy riding plus sustained and peak power tests.

- Sub-threshold time trial. A controlled effort to test the aerobic engine.

- 3 minute/1 minute/max efforts. Checking the high end.

Week 1	Rest/test
Week 2	Work
Week 3	Work
Week 4	Work
Week 5	Rest/test
Week 6	Work
Week 7	Work
Week 8	Work
Week 9	Rest/test
Week 10	Work
Week 11	Work
Week 12	Rest/test

9 work weeks

These building weeks include rest days, hard intervals, a sprint session and either your favorite ride or a devious all-in-one workout.

- Red intervals. You will warm up with sweet spot intensity (you did a ton of this in Pump Up the Base), then you'll be banging out longer and longer intervals way above your comfort zone.

- Sprints. Level 2 base with full-on sprints mixed in.

- The Kitchen Sink. This is the A-1 mandatory workout for all riders because it works all your energy systems. If you can't go for a real ride, rock this.

Keep in mind you are a mountain biker — an athlete — not hamster on a wheel. You will never, ever, just sit there and crank. You will always pay attention to technique. For some powerful pedaling tips and drills, see Pump Up the Base. For other skills tips, see Mastering Mountain Bike Skills and Teaching Mountain Bike Skills.

The goal, as always: Help you ride better, farther and faster — without beating you down or compromising your job, family or body.

Mastering Mountain Bike Skills

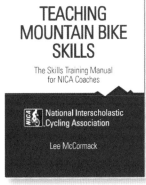

Teaching Mountain Bike Skills

You are your coach. Pay attention to how you feel and perform. Tweak this system to fit your life.

If you have a professional coach, that's ideal because he or she will tailor a training program specifically to your needs. Encourage your coach to incorporate some elements of this program. Several pro coaches are using Pump Up the Base with their clients.

REST/TEST WEEKS

The work weeks (and especially the red intervals) are going to be very effective, but they will be taxing. You're only going to do two or three work weeks in a row, then have a rest/test week.

Why a rest/test week?

We want you to get better and stronger, not more tired and bitter. You'll need a rest.

The tests shown here give you good intensity work without a huge training load. They keep you sharp, and they tell you how you're doing.

Use your test results to tweak your workout intensities, get stoked about your progress or, if you're losing power, to get way more rest.

A mellow solo ride is a great way to build endurance, recover from a hard training cycle and GET STOKED! Doug Cutter enjoys Medicine Bow Mountain, WY. Photo by yannphotovideo.com

When will I be doing rest/test weeks?

Ideally, you'll do one rest/test week before you start this program, then one every 2-3 weeks. Here's your overall 12-week mission:

Week 1	Rest/test
Week 2	Work
Week 3	Work
Week 4	Work
Week 5	Rest/test
Week 6	Work
Week 7	Work
Week 8	Work
Week 9	Rest/test
Week 10	Work
Week 11	Work
Week 12	Rest/test

During each rest/test week you will do a lot of easy riding (and hopefully some strength training), plus two targeted workouts/tests:

Special workout 1: Sub-max time trial

Purpose:

Check your aerobic fitness. Get in a nice workout.

Protocol:

- Warm up

- 20-40 minutes at 90% of threshold power. This is sweet spot intensity: A good measure of fitness (and some quality work) but not a soul-crushing effort.

- Cool down

I live at the top of a 2.5-mile, 1,200 foot climb. That's a perfect power test. When I started training like this, I could do the climb in about 29 minutes. My new record is under 18 minutes (despite an older body and way less riding time). That's the benefit of targeted training and improved pedaling technique.

Submax time trial

Ways to measure:

On your trainer with a power meter, maintain the same power and track your average heart rate.

On your trainer with a power meter, maintain the same heart rate and track your power.

Do a familiar climb at a controlled heart rate or perceived exertion. Are you going faster?

Rock your favorite mountain bike ride with a controlled heart rate or perceived exertion. Are you going faster? For a mountain biker, this is the best indicator of overall fitness and kung fu. And it's generally more fun than the trainer.

You can endure your submax time trial on the indoor trainer, but wouldn't a gradual alpine climb with your crew be more fun? Photo by yannphotovideo.com.

Special workout 2: Power testing

Mountain bikers do more than pedal. Lee tests power, skill and overall kung fu on the upper pump track at Valmont Bike Park. How many laps can you ride in three minutes — on your long-travel 29er? Photo by yannphotovideo.com.

Purpose:

Check your high-end power. Practice punching out mega (or at least kilo) watts.

Protocol:

- Warm up

- 15 minutes sweet spot with bursts mixed in.

- Three minutes as hard as you can.

- Easy about 5 minutes

- 30 seconds to 1 minute as hard as you can.

  If top speed and power is important to you (I'm talking to you gravity racers), do 30 seconds. If overall trail fu is your goal, rock 60 seconds. If you are a freak or are thirsty for knowledge (like Lee), do the one-minute test, spin five minutes easy then do the 30-second test.

- Easy about 5 minutes

- Peak power. Full sprint until you reach max power. Recover fully then repeat until your power drops 10 percent. Shoot for three strong tries.

- Cool down

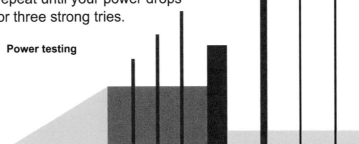

Power testing

Don't be embarrassed

This test shows your short-term and sprint power *after* you bang out other hard efforts.

You will see higher wattage if you warm up then focus solely on sprinting, but this test gives you a holistic look at your overall, real-world fitness. You generally sprint at the end of a race, right?

Lee has seen 1,500 watts when he focuses on sprint power. At the end of his first power test (sweet spot, three minutes, one minute, 30 seconds and sprint), he only had 1,050 watts in his legs. So don't feel too bad.

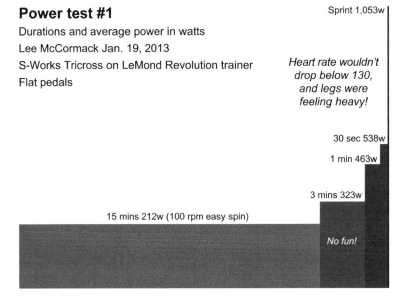

Power test #1
Durations and average power in watts
Lee McCormack Jan. 19, 2013
S-Works Tricross on LeMond Revolution trainer
Flat pedals

Sprint 1,053w

Heart rate wouldn't drop below 130, and legs were feeling heavy!

30 sec 538w

1 min 463w

3 mins 323w

15 mins 212w (100 rpm easy spin)

No fun!

Ways to measure:

A trainer or bike with a power meter is ideal. Keep track of your numbers, you nerd.

Find a section of road or trail that usually takes about 3 minutes, 1 minute or 30 seconds. Pin it. How long did it take?

Check your max speed using a cycling computer.

Sprint all-out up a hill to a certain point. How far do you coast?

The absolute numbers aren't as important as the relative measures. Are you getting strong, or are you getting tired?

Easy days

On easy days, shoot for 75 to 90 minutes of Level 2 work. That can be easy rides, non-explosive dirt jump sessions (easy gravity-aided jumps are ideal) or whatever you find fun. This is a perfect time for skills drills. How about some big figure eights at a heart rate of 120 bpm?

If you can't ride that long, do what you can. If you're an endurance racer, ride even longer.

Cruise up the hill then flow down the jumps. Lee rocks Level 2 the fun way at Valmont Bike Park in Boulder, CO. Photo by yannphotovideo.com.

24

Rest/test week – Daily workouts

Here is the basic model Lester uses with his clients. Tweak as needed to fit your life.

If you're supposed to have an easy week, take it easy! Most of us train too much (and too slow). When it's time to pin it, pin it. Otherwise lay low and let your body rebuild. Heck, take your family on a picnic.

Rest/test week
Relative intensity per day

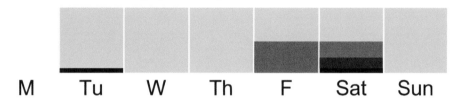

| M | Tu | W | Th | F | Sat | Sun |

Do you see all that yellow? That's a whole lot of Level 2 riding. What a great week to ride with slower friends or dial in that big jump you've been looking at.

Monday: Off

Tuesday: Level 2 with sprints (see description in work week section)

Wednesday: Level 2/easy

Thursday: Level 2/easy

Friday: Submax time trial

Saturday: Power tests. 3 minute, 1 minute, max.

Sunday: Level 2/easy but longer if possible

Get off your bike!

Hiking, skating, skiing, swimming, moto ... it's all good — especially on your Level 2/easy days.

Racing the TransAlp: Lester meets a special friend on the Austrian/Italian border. Smart training at home helps you enjoy your big adventures. Photo courtesy of Lester Pardoe.

On the trail during La Ruta: Base fitness, family time and commute!
Photo courtesy of Lester Pardoe.

WORK WEEKS

Each work week will contain some easy rides, some strength, a long base ride and hopefully a fun trail ride or DH session. It will also contain three targeted bike workouts:

- Red intervals

- Sprints

- The Kitchen Sink (if you can't ride for real)

Going red up the Valmont Bike park dual slalom track. Red intervals on the indoor trainer are efficient and measurable, but actual terrain is realistic and sweet. Photo by yannphotovideo.com.

Red intervals

In a Red workout, you will warm up then bang out 10-20 minutes of sweet spot power. This opens your aerobic system and maintains the base you built over the winter.

After the preamble, you'll perform a series of short, hard intervals. The pace will be harder than you can sustain. The rest periods will be insufficient. Your body will adapt. You will get stronger.

Sample Red workout

- 10 minutes warmup

- 10-20 minutes sweet spot with pedaling drills. (Example: 5 sitting, 5 climbing, 5 Super D. See Pump Up the Base for the drills.)

- Red intervals:
  20 seconds red, 40 seconds very easy Zone 1
  20 seconds red, 40 seconds very easy Zone 1
  20 seconds red, 40 seconds very easy Zone 1
  5-7 minutes easy Zone 1. Recover as much as you can.
  20 seconds red, 40 seconds very easy Zone 1
  20 seconds red, 40 seconds very easy Zone 1
  20 seconds red, 40 seconds very easy Zone 1
  5-7 minutes easy Zone 1. Recover as much as you can.
  20 seconds red, 40 seconds very easy Zone 1
  20 seconds red, 40 seconds very easy Zone 1
  20 seconds red, 40 seconds very easy Zone 1

- 10 minutes cool down

The sickest hour you'll ever experience!

Red intervals
30/30 3x5

Why are we doing this?

Red intervals take sweet spot intervals, which are about 8, and turn them up to 11.

- You'll be able to maintain even more power/work when you ride.

- You'll be able to recover even more quickly from hard efforts.

Most riders ride too hard on easy days and too easy on hard days. We encourage you to go easy on your easy days — and freaking pin it on your hard days. This is a hard day. But it's the key to unlocking your potential.

Unless they are specifically trying to do otherwise, most riders spend most of their riding time in Zone 3. That's a brisk, comfortable pace, and it's fine. The thing is, a lot of Zone 3 riding does these two things:

- It tires you out. Even if you're not obviously exhausted, the lingering slowness and dead legs will prevent you from accessing your top performance (and fun).

- It doesn't train you all that effectively. If you cruise a lot, you get good at cruising. Lester calls this the locomotive effect, where you get good at churning out moderate power, but you never have access to the top end.

Red intervals are hard. They take some discipline. But they are super effective. What better mid-week adventure?

Think of your Red day as the cornerstone of your training program. For the rest of the week, have fun and mix it up.

QUALITY: When your power goes down 10 percent, you are done with your red intervals. There's no sense beating yourself up unless you're going to reap the rewards of red effort.

WARNING: Red days are very effective, but they are very taxing. Only do one of these per week. Take an easy week every few weeks.

What is sweet spot intensity?

Your Red days will start with sweet spot riding. Sweet spot is a great way to build greater capacity with minimal strain (Red is a great way to build *maximum* capacity with *lots* of strain).

The sweet spot is medium-hard (or orange-red). You're not cruising (that's lower-level aerobic base), and you're not pinning it (that's higher-level anaerobic work). Sweet spot intensity takes some focus to maintain. It's not crazy difficult, but you do have to pay attention.

- If you have a power meter, sweet spot is around 91-100% of your threshold power.

- If you have a heart rate monitor, it's around 95-100% of your threshold heart rate.

- If you have lungs and a voice box, it's as hard as you can go while speaking. If you can say the entire Pledge of Allegiance, you're at the low end. If you can speak only in short sentences, you're at the high end. If you can't talk, you're going too hard.

"3 x 20 minutes at sweet spot is a hell of a lot."
— Coach Lester Pardoe

How long do I have to stay in sweet spot?

I hope you did Pump Up the Base or a similar program before this one, because the Red warmup will include 10-20 minutes at sweet spot. The last week of Pump Up the Base was 3 x 20 minutes, so no problem, right?

If you don't have a solid base, this warmup will feel like a workout.

What is red intensity?

Do you know that pace you can maintain for a while? It's pretty hard, but you can hold it if you want it badly enough. If you race a short track or cyclocross race, that's about your threshold.

This is a lot harder. If you're a general XC rider, these intervals will be at 125-130% of threshold power. If you can maintain 250 watts, you'll be pinning 312 to 325 watts.

If you're more of a power rider, say a Super D or enduro racer, try for 130-140% of your threshold power. If you can maintain 250 watts, you'll be pinning 325 to 350 watts.

If all-out power is your thing, say for downhill and gated racing, try to hold even more power. It's only for a little while. You can do fewer intervals, but make the ones you do count.

Go as hard as you can!

If you, like Lee, are a stronger sprinter than an endurance rider, your red power might be higher than the suggested 125-140% of threshold.

In his first red intervals, Lee easily held more than 200% of threshold power. That would be more impressive if his endurance power wasn't so unimpressive.

If you're over or under the suggested power level, just pin it as hard as you can while being able to finish the intervals with consistent power and form.

How easy is easy?

If you've just done a red interval, spin very easily. Just keep the pedals turning and rest as much as you can. You're about to go red again.

If you're between sets of red intervals, spin very easily — Level 1 — for 5-7 minutes. Recover as much as you can in that time.

If you're dying for more Level 2 base work, you can ride Level 2 for a while between sets of Red intervals. Heck, some technical climbs will tell you when to go red.

What if I don't have a power meter?

Go by feel. If the set calls for six intervals, and you're on number four, you should feel like six is doable but hard. Eight should seem impossible.

Use heart rate. The intervals are too short for your heart to respond at first, but after a few rounds you should be way up near red line.

Use speed. What average speed can you maintain up your local hill? Good for you. Now add 25-40 percent.

Use the old-fashioned approach. Go as hard as you can for the prescribed time, recover the best you can then do it again. Try to find your maximum functional power, ie the maximum effort level you can sustain while still being able to control your bike. This is super useful for pinning technical downhills.

When Lee was racing Super D seriously, he knew he could maintain 175 beats per minute for the whole race and peek into the 178 zone for short periods. Anything over that and he was too stupid to ride safely.

How long do I have to stay red?

In phase 1 we'll start with 20/40 intervals. For each repetition you will go red for 20 seconds, then spin easy for 40 seconds. You will start with three sets of three repetitions each. If you are riding hard enough, it will be a wonderful challenge.

In phase 2 the intervals will be 30/30. This is a lot harder.

In phase 3 the intervals will be 40/20. This is a whole other game. Way harder. But by now you'll be teaching your body to handle obscene amounts of work.

Do red intervals have to be pedaling?

No! Pedaling is the easiest, most measurable way to perform red intervals, but it's not the only way.

Pump tracks are awesome too. You get the same (or greater) work, plus you're developing total-body strength and skill. Plus it's fun.

On the pump track, pin it for a certain number of seconds or laps then cruise the off period.

During the on phase of your red pump-track intervals, strive for weightless frontsides. Push very hard down the back, pull very hard up the front. Valmont Bike Park upper pump track. Photo by yannphotovideo.com

- You have to be very skilled to flow on the track while recovering from a red effort.

- If you're a normal person, you can pin your red interval, raise your seat, spin around to recover then dive back into the track for the next interval. That's one of the great things about a remote seatpost.

- If you just can't keep riding after your on period (which is likely), walk in circles or slump on your bike until it's time to go again.

If you are a Rider (capital R), please mix it up. Do some intervals pedaling, some pumping and some just plain pinning sections of trail (safely and responsibly, of course).

As a matter of fact, these intervals do not have to be on a bike. If you're traveling or just can't be on a bike, you can do running, calisthenics or any sort of full-body circuit. Burpees are awesome! Try 10 sets of 10, on one-minute intervals.

Check out these lateral ViPR slides with Alex Willie at RallySport Health and Fitness in Boulder, CO

https://www.facebook.com/photo.php?v=10151342949839871&set=vb.623224870&type=2&theater

Do I have to do all of the intervals?

Ideally yes, but that's gonna be hard.

If your form starts to fall apart, or if your power/speed goes down 10 percent, you are done. Either give yourself more rest or call it a day. Pace yourself next time.

Penance: Do 100 burpees because you are weak!

How can I adjust this for me?

I hope this is all too easy for you, and you need to pin it harder, longer. More likely, you'll need to adjust the other way.

- Make the On period harder or easier.

- Make the On period longer or shorter.

I am special. I don't need these!

Yes, true. You are a magnificent, beautiful person.

But you should still do this.

If you hate doing red intervals, that means you really need to do them!

If you are an XC nerd or overall trail rider, use the power levels described above. This will break you out of the locomotive syndrome.

If you are a gravity rider, make even more power. Watch helmet cam footage and create virtual DS, DH and Enduro race runs.

Feel free to tweak these red intervals to suit your abilities and goals. You're going to hate this, but the more you suck at this type of riding the more you need to do it.

Red workout progression

The Red workout is the cornerstone of the system. You will reap huge benefits from it, but it's a big stress on your body, so you need to follow a progression.

"20/40 3x4" means 20 seconds hard, 40 seconds easy, three sets of four repetitions:

- Pin it for 20 seconds. Go easy for 40 seconds. That is one repetition.

- Do four repetitions. That is one set.

- Recover.

- Do another set.

- Recover.

- Do another set for a total of three sets.

This program gives you three different red-interval progressions. Unless you can prove that you are gnarly, start with Pinner.

Pinner – For most everyone

20/40 3x3
20/40 3x4
20/40 3x5

30/30 3x4
30/30 3x5
30/30 3x6

40/20 3x5
40/20 3x6

Turbo – For higher-level riders and racers

20/40 3x4
20/40 3x6
20/40 3x8

30/30 3x6
30/30 3x8
30/30 3x10

40/20 3x8
40/20 3x10

Ripper – For gravity, enduro and more power-oriented riders

15/45 3x3
15/45 3x4
15/45 3x5

20/40 3x4
20/40 3x5
20/40 3x6

30/30 3x5
30/30 3x6

Jim Kanter practices (and develops) serious sprint power at Horsetooth Mountain in Fort Collins, CO. Photo by yannphotovideo.com

Sprint workout

In the crazy world of Coach Lester Pardoe, this is one of your "easy" days. The mission is to get loose, have fun, work on some skills then pin some very short but awesomely powerful bursts.

The workout would look like:

Trainer or road bike official style

For a quick workout, do 10 minutes during each Level 2 period. If you're trying to get lots of base, rock an hour at each Level 2 period. Do whatever works for your body, schedule and goals.

- Warm up

- Level 2 riding

- 5 seconds full power/55 seconds easy Level 1 spin
  5 seconds full power/55 seconds easy Level 1 spin
  5 seconds full power/55 seconds easy Level 1 spin

- Level 2 riding

- 5 seconds full power/55 seconds easy Level 1 spin
  5 seconds full power/55 seconds easy Level 1 spin
  5 seconds full power/55 seconds easy Level 1 spin

- Level 2 riding

- 5 seconds full power/55 seconds easy Level 1 spin
  5 seconds full power/55 seconds easy Level 1 spin
  5 seconds full power/55 seconds easy Level 1 spin

- Level 2 riding

- Cool down

Easy ride with sprints

Or:

Real world fun style

Judy Freeman is a pro XC racer for the crankbrothers Race Club, and she knows the importance of on-bike functional power/skill training. Here she gets perfectly weightless on the Valmont Bike Park upper pump track. This requires (and develops) serious Level 7 power. Photo by yannphotovideo.com

Go for a fun, Level 2 ride. Mix in some explosive efforts:

- Sprint out of the corners.

- Hammer short, steep climbs.

- Pass your buddy.

- Ride half a pump track lap as fast as you can.

- Do something amazing on a BMX rhythm section.

- Practice your gate start when you roll into the dirt jumps.

- Etc.

This is the fun way. Remember, you do not have to be pedaling! Pumping, cornering and general ripping also develop neuromuscular power.

It makes a lot of sense to hone your pure sprint technique on the trainer or road, then bring it to real terrain. Few riders can actually put their full power to the ground when the ground is bumpy.

Do you hate sprinting?

Go for a long, easy ride and mix in some sprinting.

Do you hate easy rides?

Go out for some sprints and mix in some easy riding.

Why are we doing this?

The faster and more powerfully you can pedal, the more oomph you have when you need it and the easier it is to pedal at lower intensities.

As my high school strength coach used to say, in long socks and short shorts, "Anything a weak muscle can do, a strong muscle can do better."

What does that mean to me?

When it's time to sprint, you are going to pin it. Full gas — all or nothing — until you peak.

We're talking five seconds. That's it. We want high rpm and huge wattage.

Exercise physiologists refer to this intensity level as neuromuscular power.

Neuromuscular power has nothing to do with aerobic or endurance fitness. It's more like the power you see on weight lifters and dirt jumpers. How fast can your legs move? How much power can you produce, even for just a moment?

As a matter of fact, please get better at reaching your peak power sooner. An elite BMXer can hit peak power (over 1,500 watts) between a dead stop and the fifth stroke. Bam!

You're already working Level 1 at 100-something watts, the sweet spot at 200-something watts and the red zone at 300-something watts. I don't care how long you can maintain 400 watts. I want to see you bust out 1,000 watts, then recover so you can rip it on the weekend.

How easy is easy?

Easier than you think.

After each 5-second sprint, spin (or pump) very easily in Level 1 for 55 seconds.

When you're between sprint sets, you should be cruising at Level 2.

What gear? How many rpm?

Mix it up. Do some sprints from a stop, some from medium rpm and some from high rpm.

Using the three sets described above, how about:

Set 1: Medium cadence. Moderate gear from 80 rpm to 120 rpm.

Set 2: Dead stop. Easy gear from 0 rpm to 100 rpm.

Set 3: Very high cadence. Moderate gear from 100 rpm to your top speed.

Why sprint? I'm not a sprinter.

Dude, everyone should be a sprinter sometimes. These explosions are going to increase your leg speed and maximum power. You will have a quicker, smoother pedal stroke and massive power when you want it.

Do you want to clear that gnarly climb? Win that prime? Pass your buddy between corners? Jump that double right out of the start gate? Do the work.

Pro BMX Skills

But, dude, I am a sprinter.

If sprinting is important to you — BMX, 4X, slalom — you can mix up the durations to suit your event. Say 5 seconds, 15 seconds and 30 seconds.

If you're sprinting longer than 5 seconds, this is no longer an "easy" day. Adjust the rest of your week so you don't crush yourself.

For crazy detail on sprint technique and training, see the book Pro BMX Skills.

Does this have to be pedaling?

No! You are a Rider, remember? You can (and should) practice explosive movement on a pump track, BMX track, at the dirt jumps and on natural terrain.

Hey kids, dirt jumping is excellent for neuromuscular development. Tell your parents!

If you have no such terrain, how about doing a few bunny hops in a row? That's excellent power training.

Plyometrics and calisthenics count!

How about some box jumps or, our favorite, burpees?

Kitchen Sink Workout

Lester prescribes this workout for all of his clients, no matter what kind of rider or racer they are.

It works all the energy systems in a systematic and devious way. It consists of roughly:

- 10 minutes warm up

- 20-40 minutes sweet spot

- 2 x 5 minutes at threshold with five minutes rest after each effort

- 3 minutes as hard as you can, five minutes rest

- 1 minute as hard as you can, five minutes rest

- 3 x sprint full bore with 55 seconds rest after each sprint

- 10 minutes cool down

Serious business!

Kitchen Sink

Functional

If you can't get out for a sweet rip session on the weekend, rock this program on your trainer or the road.

If you can mix in some pump track, great! How about doing the longer intervals with pedals and the shorter ones with pump?

Fun

Better yet, ride your favorite trail like you mean it. Cruise the flats. Hammer the steeps. Blast out of the corners. Show your riding friends who's boss.

No wonder trail riding is the best overall prep for any mountain bike event: It mixes all of your energy systems ... plus full-body integration ... plus skills ... plus stoke!

Easy days

On easy days, shoot for 75 to 90 minutes of Level 2 work. That can be easy rides, dirt jump sessions or whatever you find fun. This is a perfect time to for skills drills. How about some big figure eights at a heart rate of 120 bpm?

If you can't ride that long, do what you can. I like pushing my twin girls around our mountain neighborhood in a stroller.

Don't forget your strength work.

Your favorite trail ride will likely cover all the elements of the Kitchen Sink workout. Tom Overton does a functional red interval (with a sprint mixed in) at Devil's Backbone in Loveland, CO.

Work week – daily workouts

Here is the basic model Lester uses with his clients. It involves less hard riding, and more easy riding, than you might expect. Lester says most athletes can only handle 1-2 tough workouts per week, week after week.

Ninety minutes for each "real" workout plus base and off-bike training totals about 9-10 hours per week, which is standard for serious/competitive adult riders.

Everything is flexible. Switch days to fit your life. If you're training for enduro, do a couple hard days on the weekend, then lay low during the week.

Work week
Relative intensity per day

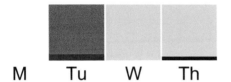 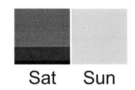

Two hard days surrounded by easy days.

M   Tu   W   Th   F   Sat   Sun

Monday: Off

Tuesday: Red intervals. This is the cornerstone of your mid-week training. It's early in the week so you have time to recover.

Wednesday: Level 2/cross train

Thursday: Level 2 with sprints

Friday: Off

Saturday: Fun/quality ride or race. If not, Kitchen Sink.

Sunday: Level 2 base. Fun but not tiring. Ride with slower people. Explore sweet new trails.

MUST-HAVE EQUIPMENT

A bike and a place to ride it.

Indoors is most measurable and time-effective. Plus it's safer when you pedal so hard you can't see straight.

Outdoors is more fun. Ultimately, that's where you need to apply your kung fu.

Indoor spin bikes are fine, especially if they have power meters.

Whatever and wherever you can ride is awesome. Just do the work!

If you have to ride at night … in the snow … on a snow bike … then go out and pin it! Chad Melis is a Colorado hero for a reason. Photo by yannphotovideo.com.

NICE-TO HAVE EQUIPMENT

A trainer or power meter that measures wattage, cadence and heart rate. This is ideal.

A bike computer and/or heart rate monitor.

A sweet trail. Mix in some pedaling, pumping and overall ripping.

Strava. This online tool uses a GPS unit or smart phone to track your rides. What a clever way to measure your climbing times, but a potentially irresponsible and dangerous way to measure downhills.

A pump track. What a great place to do some (or all) of your intervals. We're talking integrated full-body work, skills and fun.

At home Lee has been training on his Shimano Ultegra SL-equipped S-Works Tricross mounted to a LeMond Revolution trainer with the PowerPilot power meter/computer. Note the flat pedals. And how about that yoga mat!

Lee's backyard pump track surfs the contour and gains/loses 10 vertical feet per lap. Intervals on this track are hard work.

TRAINING ON A PUMP TRACK

By now you must have heard that pump tracks are rad. They are little, cheap and provide some of the most compressed skills and fitness training you can get.

Pump tracks are to kung fu as stationary trainers are to pedaling. If you are serious about Riding, you cannot merely practice pedaling. It's shocking how many racers use only traditional road-based training methods then wonder why they suck on real terrain.

Depending on your event, you should incorporate somewhere between "some" and "a lot of" pump/skills practice.

Brandon Dwight, an elite XC and CX racer, knows all about the benefits of pump track training. Here he rocks a skills clinic with Lee. Photo by yannphotovideo.com

You don't need a pump track. You can and should rip real terrain – especially if it's technical. Any tiny loop or sweet section can be used to practice cornering, pumping and pedaling (plus get the appropriate level of training stress). The most specific practice for rallying trails is … rallying trails.

BMX tracks are awesome too. They mix pedaling and pumping in a way that … well, we all know that BMXers rip.

Pedaling/skill training proportions
Every rider should work on pedaling.
Every rider should work on riding.

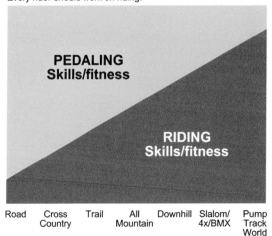

PEDALING
Skills/fitness

RIDING
Skills/fitness

Road	Cross Country	Trail	All Mountain	Downhill	Slalom/ 4x/BMX	Pump Track World Tour

Discipline

Here are some ways you can fit pump-track action into your workouts:

Sub-threshold time trials

When most people ride pump tracks, the effort is very high and anaerobic, so they can only do a few laps at a time.

If you are a highly skilled and fit rider, and you have a well-built pump track, you can pump aerobically. How many laps can you do in 20 minutes? How long does it take to ride 100 laps? Oh man, what a complete measure of strength, endurance and kung fu.

Relax, find your balance and move in phase with the track. How long can you last? Photo by yannphotovideo.com

Sweet spot efforts

If you are one of the few riders who can ride a pump track for 10-20 minutes at sweet spot effort, by all means do it.

3 minute/1 minute/30 second/max power tests

If you are a trail rider or gravity racer, there is no denser way to build or measure overall skill and fitness. Pick a number of laps that fits the amount of time you want to be working.

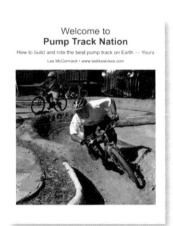

- How many laps can you ride in three minutes? How fast can you ride 10 laps?

- How many laps can you ride in one minute? How fast can you ride three laps?

- How fast can you ride one lap?

**Welcome to
Pump Track Nation**

Red intervals

Oh boy, this is going to be good.

Pick the number of laps you can ride in the desired amount of work time. It might be some fraction of a lap.

Or use a lap timer. You probably have one on your phone. Set it to beep whenever it's time to change intensity.

Pump track pro style: Pin the on phase on the pump track. Pump easy during the off phase. Repeat. If you can recover while maintaining pump flow, that is impressive!

Mortal style: Pin the on phase on the pump track, then pull off the track and spin easy. Dive back in for the next on phase, repeat.

Sprints

You can do one of your easy/sprint days at the pump track or BMX track.

When it's time to sprint, pump or pedal one section as fast as you can. Focus on insanely fast movement. This is a great time to try that new jump option.

You must see this video:
http://www.leelikesbikes.com/my-p-3-rips-the-lower-valmont-pump-track.html

Kitchen Sink

Doing the entire Kitchen Sink workout on a pump track would be a real feat of skill and fitness. YouTube that and send us the link. If you are human, how about doing the long effort on the pedals and the shorter ones on the pump?

You are not a dirt roadie. Mix up your training based on what you want to do — and what you love doing!

To practice your explosive power, try to crush your bike into a berm then hop out to backside. Photo by yannphotovideo.com

PREPARING FOR A SPECIFIC EVENT

This plan will help you get into great shape for a big ride or race, but you don't want to finish Week 11 on the week of Worlds.

The goal is to arrive at the race with enough rest to perform — but not so much rest you lose fitness.

A professional trainer like Lester will adjust your training plan to suit your goals and how your body reacts to the work. It's hard to beat that kind of attention, but you can design your own taper. Some thoughts:

Maintain your normal workout schedule. Ride days are still ride days. Off days are still off days.

Maintain intensity. Do your hard intervals just as hard as usual.

Reduce volume. Do shorter rides and fewer intervals. That's where the taper comes in. You maintain the same sharpness but reduce the overall training stress. Cut your overall volume by 50 to 60 percent.

Any one workout will give you a tiny improvement in fitness, but a good taper will give you a major improvement in performance.

Depending on how hard you've been training and how long your event is, you should taper one to three weeks. Long events need more taper. Short events need less. This sample chart shows how much you might cut volume before a race:

Event	3rd week before race	2nd week before race	Week of race
Ultra	20%	40%	60%
XC	--	30%	50%
Gravity	--	30%	50%

You can only do a thorough taper for a few key events each season. Otherwise you have to maintain your training schedule. It's very hard to race at a high level every week -- no wonder racers get so exhausted by the end of the season.

The harder you've been training, the more taper you need.

It's better to be too rested than to be too trained. That advice comes from both Brian Lopes and Ned Overend — both legends in their disciplines. If you are tired, it doesn't matter how fit you are because you can't give it everything you have. If you are rested, you can execute to your full potential.

This program is going to elevate your potential. It's your job to get enough rest — then pin it!

Gentleman warrior Greg Keller knows how to prepare for a big event. Here he punches up a steep climb at Valmont Bike Park. Check out Greg's site www.mudandcowbells.com. Photo by yannphotovideo.com

AFTER THESE 12 WEEKS

When you finish this program, you should be in pretty decent riding shape.

What next? Here are some ideas:

Just ride. Pin it on the weekends. Go on an epic riding trip. If you go "off plan," try to maintain a good balance of intensities and skills.

Go crush your race. If you timed this program with a taper then a big event, good for you. Rip it up and tell me how it goes.

Keep it up. If you like how this program feels, you can start over again. To focus your fitness in a certain direction, switch from the Pinner option to the Turbo or Ripper option. You can also create your own mini cycles: simply repeat Weeks 10, 11 and 12, or tweak the program to suit your favorite event.

- If you want to race long, increase your easy miles and cut your intensity volume (but maintain your snap).

- If you want to race short, increase your intensity work and cut your easy miles (but maintain your endurance).

At the end of your season, be sure to lay off for a while. Get some rest and do other things. Build your off-bike mobility, stability and strength. When you're ready to start building riding fitness, start with a base program like Pump Up the Base, then rock this program again.

Train hard. Get rest. Have fun!

-- Lee

There's no better place to practice trail riding … than on a trail.
Lee rails upper Hall Hanch in Lyons, CO circa 2006.

TRAINING OVERVIEW – PINNER

Who it's for: Most of us.

Note what you do and how you feel. Track the results of your tests.

Week	Monday	Tuesday	Wednesday	Thursday	Friday	Saturday	Sunday
1 - rest/test	Off	Easy/sprints	Easy	Easy	Submax TT	Power test	Easy
2 - work	Off	Red 20/40 3x3	Easy	Easy/sprints	Off	Fun/quality	Long easy
3 - work	Off	Red 20/40 3x4	Easy	Easy/sprints	Off	Fun/quality	Long easy
4 - work	Off	Red 20/40 3x5	Easy	Easy/sprints	Off	Fun/quality	Long easy
5 - rest/test	Off	Easy/sprints	Easy	Easy	Submax TT	Power test	Easy
6 - work	Off	Red 30/30 3x4	Easy	Easy/sprints	Off	Fun/quality	Long easy
7 - work	Off	Red 30/30 3x5	Easy	Easy/sprints	Off	Fun/quality	Long easy
8 - work	Off	Red 30/30 3x6	Easy	Easy/sprints	Off	Fun/quality	Long easy
9 - rest/test	Off	Easy/sprints	Easy	Easy	Submax TT	Power test	Easy
10 - work	Off	Red 40/20 3x5	Easy	Easy/sprints	Off	Fun/quality	Long easy
11 - work	Off	Red 40/20 3x6	Easy	Easy/sprints	Off	Fun/quality	Long easy
12 - rest/test	Off	Easy/sprints	Easy	Easy	Submax TT	Power test	Easy

TRAINING OVERVIEW – TURBO

Who it's for: Fit and serious XC racer types. You'll spend more time in the red zone.

Note what you do and how you feel. Track the results of your tests.

Week	Monday	Tuesday	Wednesday	Thursday	Friday	Saturday	Sunday
1 - rest/test	Off	Easy/sprints	Easy	Easy	Submax TT	Power test	Easy
2 - work	Off	Red 20/40 3x4	Easy	Easy/sprints	Off	Fun/quality	Long easy
3 - work	Off	Red 20/40 3x6	Easy	Easy/sprints	Off	Fun/quality	Long easy
4 - work	Off	Red 20/40 3x8	Easy	Easy/sprints	Off	Fun/quality	Long easy
5 - rest/test	Off	Easy/sprints	Easy	Easy	Submax TT	Power test	Easy
6 - work	Off	Red 30/30 3x6	Easy	Easy/sprints	Off	Fun/quality	Long easy
7 - work	Off	Red 30/30 3x8	Easy	Easy/sprints	Off	Fun/quality	Long easy
8 - work	Off	Red 30/30 3x10	Easy	Easy/sprints	Off	Fun/quality	Long easy
9 - rest/test	Off	Easy/sprints	Easy	Easy	Submax TT	Power test	Easy
10 - work	Off	Red 40/20 3x8	Easy	Easy/sprints	Off	Fun/quality	Long easy
11 - work	Off	Red 40/20 3x10	Easy	Easy/sprints	Off	Fun/quality	Long easy
12 - rest/test	Off	Easy/sprints	Easy	Easy	Submax TT	Power test	Easy

TRAINING OVERVIEW – RIPPER

Who it's for: Power-focused riders. Super D, enduro, downhill. The red-interval on periods are shorter, but they should be harder.

Go as hard as you can ... while still finishing all of your intervals.

Note what you do and how you feel. Track the results of your tests.

Week	Monday	Tuesday	Wednesday	Thursday	Friday	Saturday	Sunday
1 - rest/test	Off	Easy/sprints	Easy	Easy	Submax TT	Power test	Easy
2 - work	Off	Red 15/45 3x3	Easy	Easy/sprints	Off	Fun/quality	Long easy
3 - work	Off	Red 15/45 3x4	Easy	Easy/sprints	Off	Fun/quality	Long easy
4 - work	Off	Red 15/45 3x5	Easy	Easy/sprints	Off	Fun/quality	Long easy
5 - rest/test	Off	Easy/sprints	Easy	Easy	Submax TT	Power test	Easy
6 - work	Off	Red 20/40 3x4	Easy	Easy/sprints	Off	Fun/quality	Long easy
7 - work	Off	Red 20/40 3x5	Easy	Easy/sprints	Off	Fun/quality	Long easy
8 - work	Off	Red 20/40 3x6	Easy	Easy/sprints	Off	Fun/quality	Long easy
9 - rest/test	Off	Easy/sprints	Easy	Easy	Submax TT	Power test	Easy
10 - work	Off	Red 30/30 3x5	Easy	Easy/sprints	Off	Fun/quality	Long easy
11 - work	Off	Red 30/30 3x6	Easy	Easy/sprints	Off	Fun/quality	Long easy
12 - rest/test	Off	Easy/sprints	Easy	Easy	Submax TT	Power test	Easy

WEEK-BY-WEEK PLANS

The following pages give riding recommendations for each week and day. Those pages are formated for easy reading on smartphones. Perfect for the trainer!

You'll see three sets of numbers for each red workout. They go with these workout options:

Pinner   Turbo   Ripper

20/40 3x3 : 20/40 3x4 : 15/45 3x3

53

WEEK 1 - REST/TEST

Day	Do this
1	Rest
2	Easy/sprints 　Warm up 　Level 2 10-60min 　Sprint 5sec, easy 55sec. 3 sets of 3 　　Level 2 10-60min between sets 　Cool down
3	Level 2 60-90min
4	Level 2 60-90 min
5	Submax time trial 　Warm up 　Sweet spot 20-40min 　Cool down
6	Power test 　Warm up 　Sweet spot 15min 　Red 3min, easy 5min 　Red 30sec-1min, easy 5min 　Sprint 5sec, easy 55sec x 3 　Cool down
7	Level 2 120+min

WEEK 2 - WORK

Day	Do this
1	Rest

2	Red intervals
	  Warm up
	  Sweet spot 10-20min
	  Red 20/40 3x3 : 20/40 3x4 : 15/45 3x3
	  Cool down

3	Level 2 60-90min

4	Level 2 with sprints
	  Warm up
	  Level 2 10-60min
	  Sprint 5sec, easy 55sec. 3 sets of 3
	    10-60min Level 2 between sets
	  Cool down

5	Rest

6	Ride or Kitchen Sink:
	  Warm up
	  Sweet spot 20-40min
	  Threshold 5min, easy 5min x 2
	  Red 3min, easy 5min
	  Red 1min, easy 5min
	  Sprint 5sec, easy 55sec. x 3
	  Cool down

7	Level 2 120+min

WEEK 3 - WORK

Day	Do this
1	Rest
2	Red intervals 　Warm up 　Sweet spot 10-20min 　Red 20/40 3x4 : 20/40 3x6 : 15/45 3x4 　Cool down
3	Level 2 60-90min
4	Level 2 with sprints 　Warm up 　Level 2 10-60min 　Sprint 5sec, easy 55sec. 3 sets of 3 　　10-60min Level 2 between sets 　Cool down
5	Rest
6	Ride or Kitchen Sink: 　Warm up 　Sweet spot 20-40min 　Threshold 5min, easy 5min x 2 　Red 3min, easy 5min 　Red 1min, easy 5min 　Sprint 5sec, easy 55sec. x 3 　Cool down
7	Level 2 120+min

WEEK 4 - WORK

Day	Do this
1	Rest
2	Red intervals Warm up Sweet spot 10-20min Red 20/40 3x5 : 20/40 3x8 : 15/45 3x5 Cool down
3	Level 2 60-90min
4	Level 2 with sprints Warm up Level 2 10-60min Sprint 5sec, easy 55sec. 3 sets of 3 10-60min Level 2 between sets Cool down
5	Rest
6	Ride or Kitchen Sink: Warm up Sweet spot 20-40min Threshold 5min, easy 5min x 2 Red 3min, easy 5min Red 1min, easy 5min Sprint 5sec, easy 55sec. x 3 Cool down
7	Level 2 120+min

WEEK 5 - REST/TEST

Day	Do this
1	Rest
2	Easy/sprints Warm up Level 2 10-60min Sprint 5sec, easy 55sec. 3 sets of 3 Level 2 10-60min between sets Cool down
3	Level 2 60-90min
4	Level 2 60-90 min
5	Submax time trial Warm up Sweet spot 20-40min Cool down
6	Power test Warm up Sweet spot 15min Red 3min, easy 5min Red 30sec-1min, easy 5min Sprint 5sec, easy 55sec x 3 Cool down
7	Level 2 120+min

WEEK 6 - WORK

Day	Do this
1	Rest

2	Red intervals
	   Warm up
	   Sweet spot 10-20min
	   Red 30/30 3x4 : 30/30 3x6 : 20/40 3x4
	   Cool down

3	Level 2 60-90min

4	Level 2 with sprints
	   Warm up
	   Level 2 10-60min
	   Sprint 5sec, easy 55sec. 3 sets of 3
	      10-60min Level 2 between sets
	   Cool down

5	Rest

6	Ride or Kitchen Sink:
	   Warm up
	   Sweet spot 20-40min
	   Threshold 5min, easy 5min x 2
	   Red 3min, easy 5min
	   Red 1min, easy 5min
	   Sprint 5sec, easy 55sec. x 3
	   Cool down

7	Level 2 120+min

WEEK 7 - WORK

Day	Do this
1	Rest
2	Red intervals Warm up Sweet spot 10-20min Red 30/30 3x5 : 30/30 3x8 : 20/40 3x5 Cool down
3	Level 2 60-90min
4	Level 2 with sprints Warm up Level 2 10-60min Sprint 5sec, easy 55sec. 3 sets of 3 10-60min Level 2 between sets Cool down
5	Rest
6	Ride or Kitchen Sink: Warm up Sweet spot 20-40min Threshold 5min, easy 5min x 2 Red 3min, easy 5min Red 1min, easy 5min Sprint 5sec, easy 55sec. x 3 Cool down
7	Level 2 120+min

WEEK 8 - WORK

Day	Do this
1	Rest
2	Red intervals Warm up Sweet spot 10-20min Red 30/30 3x6 : 30/30 3x10 : 20/40 3x6 Cool down
3	Level 2 60-90min
4	Level 2 with sprints Warm up Level 2 10-60min Sprint 5sec, easy 55sec. 3 sets of 3 10-60min Level 2 between sets Cool down
5	Rest
6	Ride or Kitchen Sink: Warm up Sweet spot 20-40min Threshold 5min, easy 5min x 2 Red 3min, easy 5min Red 1min, easy 5min Sprint 5sec, easy 55sec. x 3 Cool down
7	Level 2 120+min

WEEK 9 - REST/TEST

Day	Do this
1	Rest

2	Easy/sprints
	  Warm up
	  Level 2 10-60min
	  Sprint 5sec, easy 55sec. 3 sets of 3
	    Level 2 10-60min between sets
	  Cool down

3	Level 2 60-90min
4	Level 2 60-90 min

5	Submax time trial
	  Warm up
	  Sweet spot 20-40min
	  Cool down

6	Power test
	  Warm up
	  Sweet spot 15min
	  Red 3min, easy 5min
	  Red 30sec-1min, easy 5min
	  Sprint 5sec, easy 55sec x 3
	  Cool down

7	Level 2 120+min

WEEK 10 - WORK

Day	Do this
1	Rest

2	Red intervals
	  Warm up
	  Sweet spot 10-20min
	  Red 40/20 3x5 : 40/20 3x8 : 30/30 3x5
	  Cool down

3	Level 2 60-90min

4	Level 2 with sprints
	  Warm up
	  Level 2 10-60min
	  Sprint 5sec, easy 55sec. 3 sets of 3
	    10-60min Level 2 between sets
	  Cool down

5	Rest

6	Ride or Kitchen Sink:
	  Warm up
	  Sweet spot 20-40min
	  Threshold 5min, easy 5min x 2
	  Red 3min, easy 5min
	  Red 1min, easy 5min
	  Sprint 5sec, easy 55sec. x 3
	  Cool down

7	Level 2 120+min

WEEK 11 - WORK

Day	Do this
1	Rest

2	Red intervals
	  Warm up
	  Sweet spot 10-20min
	  Red 40/20 3x6 : 40/20 3x10 : 30/30 3x6
	  Cool down

3	Level 2 60-90min

4	Level 2 with sprints
	  Warm up
	  Level 2 10-60min
	  Sprint 5sec, easy 55sec. 3 sets of 3
	    10-60min Level 2 between sets
	  Cool down

5	Rest

6	Ride or Kitchen Sink:
	  Warm up
	  Sweet spot 20-40min
	  Threshold 5min, easy 5min x 2
	  Red 3min, easy 5min
	  Red 1min, easy 5min
	  Sprint 5sec, easy 55sec. x 3
	  Cool down

7	Level 2 120+min

WEEK 12 - REST/TEST

Day	Do this
1	Rest

2	Easy/sprints
	    Warm up
	    Level 2 10-60min
	    Sprint 5sec, easy 55sec. 3 sets of 3
	        Level 2 10-60min between sets
	    Cool down

3	Level 2 60-90min
4	Level 2 60-90 min

5	Submax time trial
	    Warm up
	    Sweet spot 20-40min
	    Cool down

6	Power test
	    Warm up
	    Sweet spot 15min
	    Red 3min, easy 5min
	    Red 30sec-1min, easy 5min
	    Sprint 5sec, easy 55sec x 3
	    Cool down

7	Level 2 120+min

Printed in Great Britain
by Amazon